The Messenger of Satan

The Messenger of Satan

by
Charles Capps

06 05 04 03 10 9 8 7

The Messenger of Satan
ISBN 0-961875-6-2 (previously ISBN# 0-89274-633-5)
Copyright © 1993 by Charles Capps
P. O. Box 69
England, Arkansas 72046

Published by Capps Publishing
P. O. Box 69
England, Arkansas 72046

Contents

1

Truth About Deception

God's Word tells us that Satan is both a deceiver and a liar and the truth is not in him. (2 Thess. 2:9,10; Rev. 12:9; John 8:44.) He would like for us to believe that he is all powerful but the truth is his power is limited to his deception.

Satan takes Scripture out of context in his effort to deceive people into believing it is not God's will for them to be saved, healed, blessed or prosperous here on earth. His ultimate deception is to present truth as error and error as truth, for either will hold you in bondage.

But Jesus gave us the key to freedom from this kind of bondage in John 8:31,32 ...**If ye continue in my word, then are ye my disciples indeed; And ye shall know the truth, and the truth shall make you free.**

The apostle Paul said,

Study to shew thyself approved unto God, a workman that needeth not to be ashamed, rightly dividing the word of truth.

2 Timothy 2:15

But foolish and unlearned questions avoid, knowing that they do gender strifes.

And the servant of the Lord must not strive; but be gentle unto all men, apt to teach, patient,

In meekness instructing those that oppose themselves; if God peradventure will give them repentance to the acknowledging of the truth;

7

**And that they may recover themselves out of the
snare of the devil, who are taken captive by him at his
will.**

verses 23-26

There are many people today who are unaware that
they are opposing themselves by what they believe.
Being willing to accept truth and believe the Gospel is
the cure for deception.

Beware of False Truths

I want to expose some ideas and some beliefs, that
oppose the well being of many people who tend to read
things between the lines that are not in the context of the
Scriptures.

The thought may have originated when they read
certain Scriptures in the Bible, but we shouldn't fall for
what I call "false truths." A false truth is a statement
that is in the Bible that has been accurately recorded but
when used or quoted out of context it is not true at all. It
was true in the situation stated but quoted out of
context it is a false statement.

This is how many people are deceived and it causes
lots of problems in their lives; they take Scripture out of
its context. For instance, it's true the apostle Paul made
the statement in Romans 8:28: **...all things work
together for good....** But that statement is true only
when kept in the context of the other things that Paul
said in the preceding verses; otherwise, it is a false
statement because all things don't, always, work
together for good. Yet, many people believe they do;
therefore, they fail to resist what the devil brings against
them. They are convinced it is God's way of working

things for their good and that is not always the case. Although the statement conveys *a truth*, it is not *the truth* when used as a completed statement by itself.

We could say about any statement in the Bible: it is true that it is recorded in the Bible, but it is not necessarily the truth quoted out of context. For there are lies recorded in the Bible. The Spirit of God inspired the writer to include in the Scriptures some lies that people told, so we would know the truth about their spiritual condition. It is also a warning to us not to follow in their footsteps.

Ananias and Sapphira said, "Yes, we sold the land for so much." But they didn't sell the land for that amount. That statement was a lie. (Acts 5:1-5.)

It is true that they said that, and it is accurately recorded in the Bible; but what they said was not true at all. You will find there are other statements in the Bible recorded in the same manner. These are given by inspiration of God for reproof, for correction and for instruction in righteousness. As Paul said in Second Timothy 3:16, **All scripture is given by inspiration of God, and is profitable for doctrine, for reproof, for correction, for instruction in righteousness.**

Instruct Those Who Oppose Themselves

Notice what Paul said in Second Timothy 2:25, **In meekness instructing those that oppose themselves....** There are many good Christians — and I'm talking about people who love God with all their heart — *who oppose themselves by the way they talk, the way they believe and by the way they act.*

Paul said to instruct them. He didn't say to get mad at them. He didn't say to get in strife over it. We shouldn't get in strife because someone doesn't believe what we believe.

We have to remember that we were there one time. We didn't always believe what we believe now. Some of you reading this book won't have the same belief when you have finished reading it, for the entrance of the Word brings light. (Ps. 119:130.) When you understand that, you will have mercy on other people who don't understand it now.

We shouldn't put people down because they don't agree with the Word, for many of them just can't see it right now. When you come out of a dark building into the sunlight you have to squint because your eyes have been accustomed to darkness. When exposed to bright light, you have to squint for a while until your eyes become adjusted to greater light.

Sunday School Ideas

This is what happens to people who have been raised in religious tradition. They have, what I call, Sunday school ideas. Ideas they got from going to Sunday school that didn't exactly agree with the Bible. We've all had some Sunday school ideas that didn't agree with the Bible.

We acquired some of them by reading between the lines. We all read between the lines at times. And, if you don't have your *mind renewed* to the Word of God, *you will read the wrong thing between the lines.* That's why it is so important to renew your mind to the Word of God. *We must get to the point where we think like God*

10

thinks, walk like God walks, talk like God talks and act like God acts. We are not trying to be God, but we should learn to act as God would act in a similar situation. Paul told Timothy to instruct those that oppose themselves (2 Tim. 2:25), and that instruction comes from the Word of God.

Knowledge of the Truth Sets You Free

Quite often you hear people say that Jesus said, "The truth will make you free." But that wasn't exactly what He said. That statement could be one of those false truths if you don't rightly divide it.

For instance, if you walk up to someone on the street and say to them, "You will know the truth and the truth will make you free," you may have lied to them. That person may never know the truth. It is true that that statement is in the Bible. But this is the context in which that statement is made: **...If ye continue in my word, then are ye my disciples indeed; And ye shall know the truth, and the truth shall make you free** (John 8:31,32).

You can see what a difference it makes when you put it in context. We have all been guilty of quoting only part of the Scripture. Everyone who has a Bible has the truth but the Bible won't set them free unless it abides inside of them. (John 15:7.)

So, it isn't just the truth that sets people free. It is the *knowledge of that truth* that sets people free. When you teach or preach the Word of God, you transmit knowledge and understanding of that Word to other people. That knowledge and understanding sets them free to act on God's Word.

11

Millions of people are held in bondage today because they don't know the truth. They have some areas of truth, and they have certain points along the way that are truths but in between are gaps that are filled with misunderstanding. They are defeated in life because they believe wrong; therefore, their action or reaction to things that happen to them is wrong.

Recovering Themselves

Remember what Paul said in Second Timothy 2:25,26, **instructing those that oppose themselves...that they may recover themselves out of the snare of the devil....** In other words, those who have been taken in by deception and error must be willing to change their way of thinking and recover themselves, for no one else can do it for them.

But we can teach them and in meekness instruct them in the light of God's Word. Then God's Spirit will bear witness with their spirit that it is truth. Our part is to instruct in meekness; their part is to recover themselves out of the snare of the devil.

Action Brings Reaction

James said it this way: **Submit yourselves therefore to God. Resist the devil, and he will flee from you** (James 4:7).

Notice, he didn't say the devil would flee from God. Sometimes we have prayed for God to get the devil off of us. But first, we must submit ourselves to God, then resist the devil and he will flee from us.

When I first saw this in the Word of God I really didn't believe it, even though I was reading it out of the

Bible. I said, "But, Lord, he doesn't flee from me." The Lord kept saying to me, "But My Word said he would." I finally saw my problem. God's Word said he would and I was saying he wouldn't. I was not in agreement with God or His Word. I had to renew my mind to the Word of God before I could believe what God said in His Word.

But when I became fully persuaded that the devil would flee — when I resisted him — then he did. It was the knowledge of that truth and my action upon that knowledge in faith that set me free.

2

A Thorn of Deception

Someone has so aptly stated that deception wouldn't be so deceiving if it wasn't so deceptive. Paul's thorn in the flesh is a deceptive sacred cow, so to speak, that holds many in bondage. Religious ideas about Paul's thorn have caused so many to suffer needlessly, believing they were pleasing God.

Several years ago, I was in a certain church, having gone there to preach on Sunday morning. I sat in on the pastor's Sunday school class. That was the wrong thing to do, because then I didn't feel free to preach what I felt I should preach, for it was going to plow his ground cross-ways. I learned that everything I had to say was going to be contrary to what he taught. After hearing what he taught, if I taught against it, I would have caused a lot of confusion. I didn't believe it was wisdom to do that in his church.

 The Sunday school lesson that day was on the chastening of the Lord. He said the Lord sometimes chastens us with sickness.

 I said to myself, "Self, you are going to behave and mind your own business." But then he started talking about Paul's thorn in the flesh. He said "I've been to several Bible colleges, and no professor has ever been

15

able to tell me what Paul's thorn in the flesh was, and no one knows."

Well, I had stood it about as long as I could, and I said, "Would you mind if we take what the Bible says it is?" And of course, he agreed. So I turned to Second Corinthians 12:7 and read it. **And lest I should be exalted above measure through the abundance of the revelations, there was given to me a thorn in the flesh,** *the messenger of Satan* **to buffet me, lest I should be exalted above measure.**

But he already knew what the Scripture said; he just didn't believe it because it was contrary to what he had been taught. He had been indoctrinated and his mind had been blinded by religious ideas of men.

Subtle Deception

In Second Corinthians Paul said:

> **But I fear, lest by any means, as the serpent beguiled Eve through his subtilty, so your minds should be corrupted from the simplicity that is in Christ.**
>
> 2 Corinthians 11:3

Notice that Paul didn't say, "I'm afraid, the devil is so great, he's going to defeat us in life. But, **I fear, lest by any means, as the serpent beguiled Eve through his subtilty, so your minds should be corrupted from the simplicity that is in Christ.** Jesus said it this way: *"You make the Word of God of none effect by the tradition of men."* (Matt. 15:6.) Following the tradition of men will make the Word of God ineffective in your life.

In Second Corinthians chapter twelve, we find Paul's account of his revelation and the reason why the messenger of Satan was assigned to him.

> And I knew such a man, (whether in the body, or out of the body, I cannot tell: God knoweth;)
>
> How that he was caught up into paradise, and heard unspeakable words, which it is not lawful for a man to utter.
>
> Of such an one will I glory: yet of myself I will not glory, but in mine infirmities.
>
> For though I would desire to glory, I shall not be a fool; for I will say the truth: but now I forbear, lest any man should think of me above that which he seeth me to be, or that he heareth of me.
>
> And lest I should be exalted above measure through the abundance of the revelations, there was given to me a thorn in the flesh, the messenger of Satan to buffet me, lest I should be exalted above measure.
>
> 2 Corinthians 12:3-7

The reason Paul's thorn has stuck so many people is because they have assumed that God gave it to him. It is that assumption that has kept them from putting up any resistance to that which Satan has assigned to them.

I have heard that Paul's thorn was everything from sore eyeballs to ingrown toenails. But Paul identified it as a *messenger of Satan* to buffet him.

It was not sickness, it was not sore eyeballs, or ingrown toenails. And it certainly wasn't blindness, for he was healed of that when Ananias laid hands on him in Acts 9:18. Paul identified the thorn as a messenger of Satan. He was dispatched to stir up trouble everywhere Paul preached.

Some say, "We will never know what Paul's thorn in the flesh was," as though it were hidden from us. Others say, "I don't understand why God wouldn't heal Paul."

But since Paul's thorn was not sickness or disease, it wasn't a matter of God healing Paul. It was a matter of Paul acting on the authority of God's Word to defeat the purpose of the messenger of Satan. James 4:7 says, **Submit yourselves therefore to God. Resist the devil, and he will flee from you.** James didn't say that the devil would flee from God. For it was not God's responsibility to resist him. But the devil will flee from you who are here on earth.

So if Paul didn't resist — by taking authority over this messenger of Satan — then God wouldn't. Let us say it another way, *God couldn't if Paul didn't.* Jesus couldn't do a thing about it, if Paul didn't act on the authority of God's Word.

The reason why many people don't understand what Paul's thorn in the flesh was, is that they believe God gave it to him.

But, did you notice, that the Scripture didn't say that God gave Paul the thorn in the flesh? It was an angel of the devil who was dispatched to Paul.

Yet some Bible commentaries state that God gave Paul a thorn in the flesh and it was some sort of sickness or disease to keep Paul humble. And because of that mentality, they read what the Lord's answer to Paul, **"My grace is sufficient for thee,"** was, and they assume that Jesus said, *"No Paul, I won't heal you."* (2 Cor. 12:9.)

But that wasn't what He said at all.

Notice verse seven again, **Lest I should be exalted above measure...there was given to me a thorn in the flesh...** (2 Cor. 12:7). Some have thought that Paul had too much pride because of the revelation. So God gave him a thorn in the flesh to keep him humble.

I don't believe you can find in Scripture any evidence that God had anything to do with giving Paul a thorn in the flesh. God does not give His minister a revelation of His Word and then hinder him from preaching it. That would be totally out of character with God and His Word.

The phrase, **Lest I should be exalted above measure**, is referring to the fact, that if it had not been for the messenger of Satan assigned against Paul to stir up trouble, everywhere he preached, Paul would have ~~not~~ been exalted to the point that he could have influenced the known world with this revelation. But he was not able to preach it freely, for Satan hindered him on every hand. *Not depended on the power of Christ*

Ask yourself this question: Why would God give Paul a revelation of the new birth and assign someone to cause trouble everywhere he went, so he couldn't preach that revelation? The answer is obvious, God didn't do it but Satan did.

Trouble Started at Antioch

Evidently, this messenger of Satan was assigned to Paul at Antioch. For the Scripture says, **the disciples were called Christians first in Antioch** (Acts 11:26). That is significant, because Paul spent one whole year at Antioch preaching the revelation (v. 26).

Paul taught this revelation with such effectiveness that the people began to call them Christians. No doubt, Paul shared the revelation of how the rebirth of

19

the human spirit had caused them to become new creations that never existed before. I believe the preaching of this revelation so exalted Paul's ministry in the eyes of the people that he had the potential of reaching the known world with the Gospel. For that reason Satan assigned an angel of the devil, to buffet Paul and stop this revelation.

Paul had both revival and a riot almost everywhere he preached. The riot was caused by the angel of the devil sent to stop his message. Antioch is where the persecution started, evidently it was because of the revelation Paul preached.

In John 11:47,48 when Jesus had raised Lazarus from the dead, the Pharisees and the chief priests said, **What do we? for this man doeth many miracles. If we let him thus alone, all men will believe on him....**

In Jesus' ministry the Gospel was growing to such measure, until they said everyone was turning to Him. I believe this is what Paul is referring to in essence, **Lest I should be exalted above measure. . . there was given me a thorn in the flesh.** He was saying, *"I would have been exalted above measure through this revelation even to the point that the world would have received this gospel."*

You may say, "Well, I don't know about this thorn in the flesh being an angel of the devil."

The Bible says, **...In the mouth of two or three witnesses shall every word be established** (2 Cor. 13:1). So, let's go to the eleventh chapter of Second Corinthians.

For such are false apostles, deceitful workers, transforming themselves into the apostles of Christ.

20

And no marvel; for Satan himself is transformed into an angel of light.

2 Corinthians 11:13,14

One translation says, **Satan transforms himself into an angel of light.**[1] This word "angel" is the very same Greek word that is translated "messenger" in chapter 12, verse 7, where Paul says, **...there was given to me a thorn in the flesh, the *messenger* of Satan....** So Paul is literally saying, *"There was assigned to me an angel of the devil to buffet me."*

The word "buffet" used here means to strike with a clenched fist or an open hand. In other words, it was a steady buffeting, to keep the revelation from being preached. It was not sickness and disease. **...There was given to me a thorn in the flesh, the messenger of Satan....**

So, if Paul said his thorn in the flesh was an angel of the devil, who are we to say that he was wrong? It was his thorn and he ought to have known what it was.

Religious Ideas Deceive

It is amazing that so many religious people say Paul's thorn was something other than a messenger of Satan when in the same verse that Paul mentioned it, he plainly stated what the thorn was. It is also interesting that they believe it was God who gave Paul the thorn.

---

[1] *The Worrell New Testament — A.S. Worrell's Translation With Study Notes* (published 1980 by the Gospel Publishing House, Springfield, MO 65802, and reprinted by Kenneth Hagin Ministries, P. O. Box 50126, Tulsa, OK 74150; copyright © 1904 by A. S. Worrell assigned to the Assemblies of God, Springfield, MO).

But even common sense would tell you God did not send an angel of the devil to buffet Paul. God wanted him to preach that revelation, but the devil wanted to keep him from obeying God.

Paul's statement, **the messenger of Satan to buffet me** in the *Interlinear Greek-English New Testament* states it this way, **that me *he* might buffet.**[2] A personal pronoun is used here in the Greek text. That tells us it was not sickness.

> **For this thing I besought the Lord thrice, that it might depart from me.**
>
> **And he said unto me, My grace is sufficient for thee: for my strength is made perfect in weakness. Most gladly therefore will I rather glory in my infirmities, that the power of Christ may rest upon me.**
>
> 2 Corinthians 12:8,9

My grace is sufficient for you.

What does that mean? Jesus didn't say, "No, Paul, I won't heal you," or, "No, Paul, it is not My will for you to be delivered."

The Lord said, *"My grace is sufficient for you."* In other words, God's grace was sufficient to deliver him, but Paul must act on God's Word and resist the devil.

We must understand grace before we can understand what the Lord said to Paul. We have assumed that grace was just "unmerited favor."

---

[2]*Interlinear Greek-English New Testament With a Greek-English Lexicon and New Testament Synonyms* by George Ricker Berry (Grand Rapids: Reprinted by Baker Book House, copyright © 1897 by Hines & Nobel), p. 487.

Certainly that is part of it, but there is much more to God's grace than unmerited favor.

Grace Is God's Willingness

Grace is not unmerited favor alone. What if God had said: *"I'm in favor of the world being saved, but I'm not going to get involved in it. If the world can save themselves, it's all right with Me. I'm in favor of it. But I am not going to do anything about it?"*

If God had said that, we would have been in big trouble. We would all be lost; we could not save ourselves. But God became personally involved and sent His own Son and redeemed mankind. *Grace is God's willingness to use His power and His ability on our behalf, even though we don't deserve it.*

Once you get an understanding of grace, the Bible will become a different book to you. Peter said, grace is **multiplied unto you through the knowledge of God** (2 Peter 1:2). You can't believe any further than you have knowledge. So if you don't have knowledge of what Paul's thorn in the flesh was, you can't rightly divide the Word concerning it. Therefore, that Scripture may hold you in bondage all of your life, when it really should have brought deliverance to you. That's why we are spending so much time on this subject. This is one of the most misunderstood Scriptures in the Bible.

The Lord was saying, *"Paul, My willingness to use My power and My ability on your behalf is sufficient for you. And I am willing to back you up with My ability, but you must first exercise your authority by resisting the devil."*

In other words, whatever you do on earth will be backed by heaven also. (Matt. 16:19.) But you must set it in motion by acting on the God-given authority of His Word.

Submit yourselves therefore to God. Resist the devil, and *he will flee from you* (James 4:7). If Paul didn't resist him, he wasn't going to flee. The messenger of Satan was not going to leave unless Paul resisted him. It was not God's responsibility. It was Paul's responsibility to exercise his God-given authority here on earth. Yet, it was God's anointing that Paul must rely upon for effective deliverance.

3

Paul's Thorn,
a Figure of Speech

For this thing I besought the Lord thrice, that it might depart from me.

And he said unto me, My grace is sufficient for thee: for my strength is made perfect in weakness....

2 Corinthians 12:8,9

The Lord told Paul: **"My grace is sufficient for thee: for My strength is made perfect in weakness.** When you realize that you are weak, Paul, and you can't do it within yourself, then My strength is made perfect."

In other words, *"You have to depend on My grace. The power isn't in your natural ability to get rid of this thorn."* Paul had to depend on the Holy Spirit's power and anointing for direction in the spirit.

Then Paul says, **...Most gladly therefore will I rather glory in my infirmities, that the power of Christ may rest upon me** (v. 9).

This is where people get the idea that Paul was sick, because of the word "infirmities." A hospital today is called an infirmary. That's where you put sick people. But the Greek word translated "infirmity" here means "weaknesses."[1] The words translated "weakness" and "infirmities" in Second Corinthians 12:9 are the same Greek word. Even though by implication that Greek word means "disease" and "sickness,"[2] the literal translation of both words is "weakness" ("infirmities" — "weaknesses").[3] We discussed in a previous chapter that the Scripture clearly states that Paul's thorn was a **messenger of Satan**. I believe that the word "weakness" in Second Corinthians 12:9 means weakness in the sense of not being able to do something in your own strength (no matter what type of weakness it may be) or not being able to control the situation. Paul was saying, "*I will gladly glory in my inability to control the situation.* It is not up to *me* to do it myself. I'll wait until the anointing of God comes upon me, then act accordingly." Paul is not saying that he will glory in sickness as some have supposed.

Let's approach this subject from another angle. There are several Scriptures in the Bible that refer to thorns in the side or in the eye and none of these Scriptures indicate sickness. It is just a figure of speech.

You have heard people say, "So-and-so is just a pain in the neck." Well, he isn't really a pain in the neck. That's just a figure of speech. That means he gives you trouble.

---

[1]*Interlinear Greek-English New Testament*, p. 487.

[2]James Strong, "Greek Dictionary of the New Testament," *The Exhaustive Concordance of the Bible*, (Nashville: Abingdon, 1890), p. 16, #769.

[3]*Interlinear Greek-English New Testament*, p. 487.

People Are the Thorns, Not Sickness

Let's look at Numbers 33, where God is speaking to the children of Israel.

> But if ye will not drive out the inhabitants of the land from before you; then it shall come to pass, that those which ye let remain of them shall be *pricks* in your eyes, and *thorns* in your sides, and shall vex you in the land wherein ye dwell.
>
> Numbers 33:55

Pricks in your eyes, and *thorns in your side.* Here, you can see He is talking about people. He is not talking about a sickness. The *people* that you don't cast out of the land will become thorns in your side. This is only a figure of speech.

Look now at Joshua, the twenty-third chapter.

> Know for a certainty that the Lord your God will no more drive out any of these nations from before you; but they shall be snares and traps unto you, and scourges in your sides, and *thorns* in your eyes, until ye perish from off this good land which the Lord your God hath given you.
>
> Joshua 23:13

God is telling them, *"If you don't drive them out, they will become thorns in your eyes."* Here again it is a figure of speech.

In Judges, the second chapter, we also have a reference to a thorn, yet in none of these instances does the Word indicate sickness or disease.

> And ye shall make no league with the inhabitants of this land; ye shall throw down their altars: but ye have not obeyed my voice: why have ye done this?

Wherefore I also said, I will not drive them out from before you; but they shall be as *thorns* in your sides, and their gods shall be a snare unto you.

Judges 2:2,3

Here again you can see it is used in reference to people. They will become thorns in your sides. So we see that when the Scriptures refer to a thorn in the flesh it never once refers to sickness. There is no scriptural basis for the belief that Paul was referring to any kind of sickness.

Ye know how through infirmity of the flesh I preached the gospel unto you at the first.

And my temptation which was in my flesh ye despised not, nor rejected....

Galatians 4:13,14

Here, Paul refers to infirmity of the flesh and temptation in the flesh. The Greek word used for "infirmity" is the same Greek word that is used for "weakness" in Second Corinthians 12:9.[4] The Greek word for "temptation" means any kind of temptation or trial.[5] I believe he is referring to the things he suffered for the Gospel's sake recorded in Second Corinthians 11:23-28. It is certain that the things he suffered would make one weak.

Some say Paul was sick all of his life. Some say he could just barely see and that he had all kinds of physical problems. But if you study the New Testament,

---

[4]*The Exhaustive Concordance of the Bible,* Greek Dictionary, p. 16, #769. *Interlinear Greek-English New Testament,* p. 496.

[5]See W.E. Vine, *An Expository Dictionary of New Testament Words* (Old Tappan: Fleming H. Revell, 1966), p. 117.

you'll find that Paul traveled over most of the known world twice in his missionary journeys and wrote two-thirds of the New Testament. One thing stands out in his writings, you never find a Scripture where he said he was sick. He probably did have some physical problems at times, but if he did, he never talked about them.

Some say that Galatians 4:15 proves that Paul was nearly blind.

> **Where is then the blessedness ye spake of? for I bear you record, that, if it had been possible, ye would have plucked out your own eyes, and have given them to me.**
> Galatians 4:15

Here again Paul uses a figure of speech; much the same way people today say, *"That will cost you an arm and a leg"* or *"I would give you my right arm."* This figure of speech only revealed their willingness to assist him.

Yet, some get sidetracked by what Paul said in Galatians 6:11, **Ye see how large a letter I have written unto you with mine own hand.**

Some people try to explain this statement by saying that Paul's thorn in the flesh was partial blindness. Therefore he had to make large letters for his words. But the Scripture reveals that Paul was healed of blindness.

You may ask, then why would Paul make such a statement? For we know that he wrote several larger epistles. There are at least two reasons for that statement.

First, he had written this letter with his own hand. Many of the other epistles were written by someone else, as Paul dictated the letter. This is a more believable explanation than the one that says, Paul was so blind that he had to write real large letters so he could see them. For in Paul's day, all writing was done in capital letters about an inch high. If he had to write any larger to see them, he would have been so blind that he couldn't see at all. There is nothing in the Scriptures to back the claim of Paul's supposed blindness. But to the contrary, we have proof of him being healed of blindness when Ananias prayed for him in Acts 9:17.

Dake, in his summary of the book of Hebrews, gives us probably the most valid reasons why Paul spoke of Galatians as a large letter. "Eusebius, the father of church history, explains that Paul wrote the epistle in Hebrew, leaving his name off so that it would be read and received more readily by Jews who hated him and would not want to listen to anything he had to say.... In the oldest manuscripts the epistle (Hebrews) follows Galatians with the title *To the Hebrews*, indicating that it was part of the Galatian letter. If this is true, the authorship stated in Galatians 1:1 applies to both books. This would explain why Paul speaks of Galatians as a large letter (6:11)."[6]

God's Grace Is More Than Enough

Concerning his inability to control the situation — the riots and the things that happened where he preached — Paul said, "I will glory in the fact that I can't do anything about it within myself, that the power of Christ may rest upon me." If Paul had said, "I don't

---

[6]See Finis Jennings Dake, *Dake's Annotated Reference Bible*, Twelfth Printing (Lawrenceville, Georgia: Dake Bible Sales, Inc., 1961).

need any help. I can do this job all by myself," God would have let him do his own thing, but the anointing of God would not have come upon him. He would have been fighting a fleshly battle. But Paul was the one who wrote to the Church and said,

The weapons of our warfare are not carnal, but mighty through God to the pulling down of strong holds.
2 Corinthians 10:4

With that thought in mind we can more readily understand this statement:

Therefore I take pleasure in infirmities (this is the same Greek word translated "weakness" in verse 9), **in reproaches, in necessities, in persecutions, in distresses for Christ's sake: for when I am weak, then am I strong.**

2 Corinthians 12:10

Let's look at this from a little different perspective and it will help us understand it. Paul says, "When I am weak, then am I strong." *Some say it was sickness that Paul was talking about. So let's put the word "sickness" here instead of the word "infirmity" and see if it fits.*

Therefore I take pleasure in *sickness*, **in reproaches, in necessities, in persecutions, in distresses for Christ's sake: for when I am** *sick*, **then am I** *strong*.

You can see "sickness" doesn't fit in that sentence. So we know Paul is not saying, "When I feel the worst is when I feel my best."

We can see that Paul is not talking about sickness but his inability to control the situation himself. Paul couldn't control every situation so he put his trust in the anointing of God. He used his authority and trusted God's ability.

Depend on God's Ability

Here is the way I would paraphrase what Paul said in Second Corinthians 12:10, "I'll glory in the fact that I can't handle this myself, and wait on the anointing to rise up in me and give me direction of what to do and how to do it."

We can't handle everything ourselves. But we are not in ourselves; we are in Christ and the greater One is in *us*.

Paul understood the power and the anointing of the Holy Spirit that flowed through him, so he waited on God to give specific direction before he acted on his authority.

We make a mistake when we, through the flesh, try to straighten out someone who is causing us problems because the problem is not that person but the spirit that is driving that person.

When we can't handle a situation ourselves, we can also glory in the fact that we can't correct the situation and trust God's anointing to come upon us at the appropriate time. When God's anointing comes, then we are well able, because his grace is *sufficient*.

In Ephesians 6:10, Paul said, **be strong in the Lord, and in the power of his might.** Not strong in yourself, not strong in your own fleshly impulses, but strong in the Lord, and in the power of His might, which is His anointing.

Paul — through his weakness — became strong in the Lord by depending on the anointing of the Holy Spirit within him.

4

Understanding Paul's Persecution

Beloved, think it not strange concerning the fiery trial which is to try you, as though some strange thing happened unto you:

But rejoice, inasmuch as ye are partakers of Christ's sufferings; that, when his glory shall be revealed, ye may be glad also with exceeding joy.

1 Peter 4:12,13

We should not think it to be a strange thing, that Satan would send fiery trials against us in this life to hinder us from serving and obeying God for he is an enemy of God and man.

Peter is talking about religious persecution. Certainly, we should be willing to suffer persecution, if necessary to promote the Gospel. Yes, we can rejoice even when being persecuted. But we don't rejoice because of it. For it is Satan who sends trials, tests and temptations to steal, kill and destroy. (Mark 4:15-19; John 10:10.)

First we should be sensitive to the Holy Spirit, then exercise our authority over Satan with persistent resistance. (James 4:7.)

Paul Suffered for Using the Name of Jesus

But the Lord said unto him, Go thy way: for he is a chosen vessel unto me, to bear my name before the Gentiles, and kings, and the children of Israel:

For I will shew him how great things he must suffer for my name's sake.

Acts 9:15,16

There are some who read between the lines and say, "The Lord said it was His will that the apostle Paul suffer." No, it was not God's purpose or intent that Paul suffer. But God knew that what He had called him to do would bring religious persecution. God said it because of His foreknowledge and not because of His will or intent. In other words, Jesus was saying, *"I'm going to show Paul how much he will suffer when he begins to use My name to heal the sick, cast out demons and destroy the work of the devil."* Religious persecution came against him because he preached Jesus was the Christ and used Jesus' name to do the *miracles.*

Disciples Called Christians At Antioch

Then departed Barnabas to Tarsus, for to seek Saul:

And when he had found him, he brought him unto Antioch. And it came to pass, that a whole year they assembled themselves with the church, and taught much people. And the disciples were called Christians first in Antioch.

Acts 11:25,26

Paul preached at Antioch and it doesn't mention anything about persecution until he had preached his revelation for a whole year. Because of his preaching, Antioch became a missionary headquarters for evangelism.

The disciples were called "Christians" first at Antioch. Paul taught them how they were new creatures in Christ, how they were delivered from the authority of darkness and translated into the kingdom

34

of God. Paul, writing to Timothy, refers to the persecution which started in Antioch.

> **But thou hast fully known my doctrine, manner of life, purpose, faith, longsuffering, charity, patience,**
>
> **Persecutions, afflictions, which came unto *me at Antioch*, at Iconium, at Lystra; what persecutions I endured: but out of them all the Lord delivered me.**
>
> 2 Timothy 3:10,11

This is where Paul's real persecution started: when he began to preach the revelation that we are joint-heirs of Christ, that we were no more servants but sons, capable of operating in the same anointing.

One statement stands out above all the persecution he suffered: **But out of them all the Lord delivered me.**

The Buffeting Continued

Again, in Acts, the thirteenth chapter, Paul returned to Antioch and had great success, but the buffeting continued.

> **But the Jews stirred up the devout and honorable women, and the chief men of the city, and raised persecution against Paul and Barnabas, and expelled them out of their coasts.**
>
> **But they shook off the dust of their feet against them, and came unto Iconium.**
>
> **And the disciples were filled with joy, and with the Holy Ghost.**
>
> Acts 13:50-52

Paul was in a situation again where this angel of the devil stirred up trouble. They departed and shook off the dust of their feet against them. Then in Iconium, many believed, both Jew and Greek. But the messenger of Satan was still buffeting him in Acts 14.

But the unbelieving Jews stirred up the Gentiles, and made their minds evil affected against the brethren.

Long time therefore abode they speaking boldly in the Lord, which gave testimony unto the word of his grace, and granted signs and wonders to be done by their hands.

But the multitude of the city was divided: and part held with the Jews, and part with the apostles.

And when there was an assault made both of the Gentiles, and also of the Jews with their rulers, to use them despitefully, and to stone them,

They were ware of it, and fled unto Lystra and Derbe, cities of Lycaonia, and unto the region that lieth round about:

And there they preached the gospel.

And there sat a certain man at Lystra, impotent in his feet, being a cripple from his mother's womb, who never had walked:

The same heard Paul speak: who stedfastly beholding him, and perceiving that he had faith to be healed,

Said with a loud voice, Stand upright on thy feet. And he leaped and walked.

Acts 14:2-10

Every time the messenger of Satan stirred up trouble, Paul would go to another place and the anointing of God would come upon him. Remember what Paul said, "I will glory in my weakness, in the fact that I can't control the situation." But when the anointing of God came on him, he destroyed the work of the devil.

I imagine the devil wanted to know why the buffeting had not stopped Paul. It was because Paul was operating in the power of the Spirit, not his own strength.

Man in Likeness of God

And when the people saw what Paul had done, they lifted up their voices, saying in the speech of Lycaonia, The gods are come down to us in the likeness of men.

Acts 14:11

When they saw the power of God in operation they said the gods had come down. But they had it just exactly backwards. It was not gods that had come in the likeness of men, *it was man who had come in the likeness of God.*

Death — No Match for the Anointing

And there came thither certain Jews from Antioch and Iconium, who persuaded the people, and, having stoned Paul, drew him out of the city, supposing he had been dead.

Acts 14:19

If religious people stoned him and left him for dead, you can rest assured he was dead.

Howbeit, as the disciples stood round about him, he rose up, and came into the city: and the next day he departed with Barnabas to Derbe.

Acts 14:20

Now, you see what Paul was referring to when he said, "I'll gladly glory in my weakness. For the anointing of God will come on me, *and when I am weak, then am I strong* (in the anointing of God)."

It was quite evident Paul wasn't controlling every situation. But when the disciples stood around him, he rose up. They were no doubt praying in the Spirit (Rom. 8:26-28), for what they prayed brought Paul back to life, and he departed the next day with Barnabas to Derbe and continued to preach the Gospel.

This messenger of Satan stirred up trouble for Paul every place he preached. Paul tells us that he prayed about this three times.

> **For this thing I besought the Lord thrice, that it might depart from me.**
>
> **And he said unto me, My grace is sufficient for thee....**
>
> 2 Corinthians 12:8,9

When the Lord said that to Paul, it is clear that Paul did not understand the Lord's answer at first, for he prayed again and again that it might depart from him. Every time he prayed, he kept getting the same answer: *"Paul, My grace is sufficient for you."*

Now let's answer this question: Why wouldn't or why couldn't God cause the messenger of Satan to depart from him?

We need to understand this point clearly for there is a fine line here.

#1 It was not God's responsibility. He had told man to subdue the earth and have dominion over every creeping thing. God will not violate His Word for God cannot lie. (Gen. 1:26-28; Num. 23:19.)

#2 God couldn't cause the messenger of Satan to depart from Paul, for if he did, God would be destroying the work of the devil and He would have to violate His own Word to do that. For only people born on earth have authority to do that at this time. (John 5:26,27; 1 John 3:8b) (See author's book, *Authority In Three Worlds*.)[1]

---

[1]Charles Capps, *Authority In Three Worlds* (Tulsa: Harrison House, Inc.).

38

#3 The Scripture says all that live godly will suffer persecution. As long as he was doing the will of God by destroying the works of the devil he attracted persecution. The persecution was sent by Satan to get the Word out of him and stop him from doing God's will. **THIS IS WHY GOD COULD DELIVER PAUL OUT OF PERSECUTION BUT COULDN'T REMOVE IT FROM HIM.**

Let's say it another way: it was Paul's obedience to do God's will that attracted the messenger of Satan. (Here is where the fine line is drawn.) It was God's will for Paul to do the things that were causing the persecution. But, it was not God's will for him to be persecuted for doing the will of God.

His persecution was the will of the devil sent to stop Paul from obeying God. God sent Paul to do the work of God. This was God's purpose and intent for Paul's calling. (Gal. 1:15,16.) Persecution came to him because he was doing the will of God and Satan was trying to stop him, not because God wanted him persecuted.

God delivered him out of the persecution, so he could preach in another place. But his obedience attracted persecution there also. So, as far as God was concerned, He could not remove the persecution from Paul, but Paul could be delivered out of it, by being sensitive to the anointing of the Holy Spirit and acting on his God-given authority to destroy the works of the devil. (Gen. 1:26-28; 1 John 3:8; John 17:18; Mark 16:17,18.)

5

The Way of Escape

In the sixteenth chapter of Acts we find that Paul really begins to tap into the revelation the Lord was giving him. Every time Satan stirred up persecution and stopped Paul from ministering in a city, Paul would go to another city, and great miracles would happen there also.

It is evident that the messenger of Satan — that was assigned to Paul — was unable to do all that he had been assigned to do. He just couldn't pull it off; he couldn't stop Paul from preaching the revelation God gave him.

Paul Waits for Direction

We see in Acts 16 that Paul had learned to wait on the direction and anointing of God.

> And it came to pass, as we went to prayer, a certain damsel possessed with a spirit of divination met us, which brought her masters much gain by soothsaying:
>
> The same followed Paul and us, and cried, saying, These men are the servants of the most high God, which shew unto us the way of salvation.
>
> Acts 16:16,17

Notice there was nothing really wrong with what this woman said. *She was telling the truth;* they were the servants of the most high God and they were showing the way of salvation. But who wants a demon witnessing for you?

The Demon Told the Truth

The devil never tells the truth unless it is to his advantage to do so. This demon was telling the truth so it would make her look good in the eyes of the people, for she was a fortuneteller. This familiar spirit she had, knew Paul. They understood what he had come there to do, and he evidently decided that if they couldn't stop Paul, he would at least try to get in on the deal.

We find in Paul's ministry that he faced many situations which he could not control within himself, yet the grace of God was sufficient to put him over. When Paul couldn't do it, he made a demand on the anointing of God.

The Scripture says this woman followed Paul:

> ...and cried, saying, These men are the servants of the most high God, which shew unto us the way of salvation.
>
> And this did she many days. But Paul, being grieved, turned and said to the spirit, I command thee in the name of Jesus Christ to come out of her. And he came out the same hour.
>
> Acts 16:17,18

Wisdom and Anointing

The woman followed him around for days. He knew by the Spirit of God that she was possessed by a spirit of divination. But he couldn't slap her and tell her to shut up and go home; that wouldn't be very Christ-like.

Paul waited for *the anointing of God to come on him*. He was anointed to know what it was and what to do about it. I imagine these words were sounding in his ears: "Paul, My grace is sufficient for you."

But he waited for the anointing of God to give him direction. There is a timing in God's methods and God's anointing. When the anointing came upon Paul, he just turned to the spirit and said, **I command thee in the name of Jesus Christ to come out of her. And he came out the same hour** (v. 18).

Demon Dismissed From Assignment

When Paul experienced his God-given authority under the anointing of God, the demon spirit lost his assignment. This is what God was trying to get over to Paul all this time: "My grace is sufficient for you."

Grace is God's willingness. God is always willing. But it's a matter of us acting on what we know that brings results.

Even though Paul would win over one situation, another would arise. God didn't remove them from him, but *God did* deliver him out of those situations, as he acted under the anointing of the Holy Spirit.

Paul got a revelation that God's grace was His willingness to use His power and ability on his behalf.

Act On What You Know

Regardless of what kind of situation you face in life, God's grace is sufficient for your situation. God is willing to use His power, His ability on your behalf, and it is sufficient for whatever situation you face.

But you must be willing to act on what you know. This is where so many people miss it. They don't have knowledge of God's Word, so they don't have faith to act on it.

> And it came to pass, that, while Apollos was at Corinth, Paul having passed through the upper coasts came to Ephesus: and finding certain disciples,
>
> He said unto them, Have ye received the Holy Ghost since ye believed? And they said unto him, We have not so much as heard whether there be any Holy Ghost.
>
> And he said unto them, Unto what then were ye baptized? And they said, Unto John's baptism.
>
> Then said Paul, John verily baptized with the baptism of repentance, saying unto the people, that they should believe on him which should come after him, that is, on Christ Jesus.
>
> And when Paul had laid his hands upon them, the Holy Ghost came on them; and they spake with tongues, and prophesied.
>
> And all the men were about twelve.
>
> And he went into the synagogue, and spake boldly for the space of three months, disputing and persuading the things concerning the kingdom of God.
>
> But when divers were hardened, and believed not, but spake evil of that way before the multitude, he departed from them, and separated the disciples, disputing daily in the school of one Tyrannus.
>
> And this continued by the space of two years; so that all they which dwelt in Asia heard the word of the Lord Jesus, both Jews and Greeks.
>
> And God wrought special miracles by the hands of Paul.
>
> Acts 19:1-4, 6-11

Every time Paul dismissed a demon from his assignment and took authority over the situation, great victory was won.

Notice it was God who wrought special miracles by the hands of Paul. It wasn't something that Paul did by himself. Paul exercised his authority and God furnished the anointing for the miracles.

> So that from his body were brought unto the sick handkerchiefs or aprons, and the diseases departed from them, and the evil spirits went out of them.
>
> Then certain of the vagabond Jews, exorcists, took upon them to call over them which had evil spirits the name of the Lord Jesus, saying, We adjure you by Jesus whom Paul preacheth.
>
> And there were seven sons of one Sceva, a Jew, and chief of the priests, which did so.
>
> And the evil spirit answered and said, Jesus I know, and Paul I know; but who are ye?
>
> Acts 19:12-15

You can see that it is a dangerous thing for a person to try to exercise something they don't have. They were trying to act as though they had faith when they didn't even know the Word of God. They were trying to use the power of God in the name that Paul preached. The evil spirits tore the clothes off of them and they left naked and wounded.

Paul was operating under the anointing of God, but they were not. Even when Satan had dispatched a messenger — to stop the Word of God from being preached — Paul acted on his authority and God's anointing, and the messenger of Satan failed in his assignment.

Good Out of a Bad Situation

Every time the messenger of Satan moved against Paul, the end result was that God wrought great miracles as Paul exercised his authority and God's anointing.

When *some* good comes out of a bad situation, people sometimes get the wrong impression. A classic example of how people misinterpret some situations happened in my home town.

A friend of mine had a son about five years old. Every time there was a fire he wanted to follow the fire trucks to the fire. After they had done this several times, his son said, "Daddy, why does that little red truck run all over town setting those houses on fire?"

He related the house fire to the red truck, not understanding that the red truck was there trying to put out the fire and save the house.

This is how many misinterpret the hand of God's mercy in some tragic situation today. They see God come on the scene and work some good out of that situation. Then they assume that God caused the tragedy and say, "Well, the Bible says, **All things work together for good.**" That statement is in the Bible, but Paul said that concerning praying in the Spirit when we don't know how to pray. The intent of that verse was that we can expect all we prayed about in the Spirit, by the help of the Holy Spirit, will begin to work together for good. (Rom. 8:26-28.)

Although God didn't cause the tragedy, He will go to work to bring some good out of bad situations, especially if you pray in the Spirit and act on the Word of God. This is what Paul did: he acted on the Word, and God wrought victory out of a bad situation.

> And this was known to all the Jews and Greeks also dwelling at Ephesus; and fear fell on them all, and the name of the Lord Jesus was magnified.
>
> And many that believed came, and confessed, and shewed their deeds.
>
> Many of them also which used curious arts brought their books together, and burned them before all men: and they counted the price of them, and found it fifty thousand pieces of silver.
>
> So mightily grew the word of God and prevailed.
>
> Acts 19:17-20

Prevailing Word and Action

Notice, it doesn't say Paul prevailed, but *God's Word grew and prevailed*. The people were delivered from witchcraft and curious arts. (Acts 19:17-20.) Paul was strong in the Lord and in the power of His might.

In the twenty-eighth chapter of Acts, we find that Paul has been shipwrecked and escaped to the island of Melita. Paul warned them they should not sail. He perceived by the Spirit that there would be much damage to the ship and danger to their lives. But they believed the master of the ship and sailed anyway. They found themselves in a great storm. The angel of the Lord had appeared to Paul and told him, "If you all stay with the ship, there won't be any lives lost." (Acts 27:24-31.)

Paul was not only delivered from the storm, but all lives were saved. The messenger of Satan was dispatched to stir up all kinds of problems for Paul. But, because Paul was sensitive to the Spirit, God's Word and Paul's action prevailed over every situation.

47

Fire Brings Out Viper

And when Paul had gathered a bundle of sticks, and laid them on the fire, there came a viper out of the heat, and fastened on his hand.

And when the barbarians saw the venomous beast hang on his hand, they said among themselves, No doubt this man is a murderer, whom, though he hath escaped the sea, yet vengeance suffereth not to live.

Acts 28:3,4

They said, "He's a murderer, and even though he escaped the sea, he's going to die anyway." They thought this was the judgment of God.

And he shook off the beast into the fire, and felt no harm.

Howbeit they looked when he should have swollen, or fallen down dead suddenly: but after they had looked a great while, and saw no harm come to him, they changed their minds, and said that he was a god.

Acts 28:5,6

Isn't that just like some people? They believe everything bad that happens is the judgment of God. But Paul acted in faith, on the Word and shook that serpent off into the fire and felt no harm. Then they decided, *he must be a god.*

Here again, a messenger of Satan tries to destroy Paul by a venomous viper. His action of faith not only overcame the viper, but also won a great victory through a chain reaction.

Chain Reaction to Faith Action

In the same quarters were possessions of the chief man of the island, whose name was Publius; who received us, and lodged us three days courteously.

48

> And it came to pass, that the father of Publius lay sick of a fever and of a bloody flux: to whom Paul entered in, and prayed, and laid his hands on him, and healed him.
>
> So when this was done, others also, which had diseases in the island, came, and were healed.
>
> Acts 28:7-9

Paul's faith in action started a chain reaction. He shook the viper off in the fire, refusing to give place to the devil. When he did, they wanted him to pray for the chief's father, and he was healed. Then they started bringing *their sick* to be healed. God received glory and the messenger of Satan was defeated again.

Allow me to paraphrase Paul's statement, "I will glory in my weakness (in the fact that I can't control the situation) that the power of Christ may rest upon me." Yes, God's grace was sufficient to deliver him out of every situation.

Paul Is Delivered From the Thorn

Then in the twenty-eighth chapter of Acts, notice verses 30 and 31:

> And Paul dwelt two whole years in his own hired house, and received all that came in unto him,
>
> Preaching the kingdom of God, and teaching those things which concern the Lord Jesus Christ, with all confidence, no man forbidding him.

For the first time since he preached at Antioch, Paul has freedom to preach the Gospel to all that came to him, **no man forbidding him.**

There are people who say, "Paul never did get rid of the thorn in the flesh. But he did get rid of it by being

49

sensitive to the Holy Spirit and exercising his God-given authority. It was through faith and patience that he overcame the power of the messenger of Satan. I believe it was because Paul continued to act on the authority of God's Word, the messenger of Satan lost his assignment. Through God's grace and Paul's faith in action, God won great victories. *Satan lost face. The demon lost his assignment. God was exalted and glorified.*

6

Assignments Against You

Satan may have assigned a messenger of Satan against you to harass you financially, spiritually or even physically. But God's grace is sufficient to deliver you also.

God is willing to use His power and His ability on your behalf, but He is not going to do it *for* you. As the apostle Paul said to Timothy, **...they may recover themselves out of the snare of the devil...** (2 Tim. 2:26).

Yes, God furnishes the ability, but you must exercise authority over the messengers of Satan.

Persistent Resistance

You can be delivered from your thorn in the flesh, if you learn to exercise your God-given authority through God's anointing. You resist him with God's Word and by acting on the Word.

I believe many people today have a messenger of Satan sent to harass them with all kinds of problems.

And as long as they will allow it, Satan will bring all kinds of bad situations their way. But if you know the truth and act on what you know, you can be delivered out of them all. (John 8:32; 2 Tim. 3:11.)

God's willingness to use His power and His ability on your behalf — even though you don't deserve it — is sufficient. It was sufficient for Paul and it is sufficient for everyone who believes and acts on His Word in faith.

In Acts 28, Paul was supposed to be in prison. But he had rented a house and was preaching the Gospel to all that came to him.

Paul could say, "Yes, God's grace is sufficient, for out of them all the Lord has delivered me."

Don't Let the Devil Run Over You

God is willing for you to be set free from the situations that Satan has brought against you. There are times when people suffer persecution because they preach the Gospel. We should be willing to do that for the Gospel's sake if necessary. But we should resist the devil with every fiber of our being every step of the way. If you don't resist him, he won't flee. *But that is a decision you must make; God won't make it for you.*

Beyond the Call

The question is often asked, "Is it the will of God for us to live victorious? If so, why were the apostle Paul and others plagued by stonings, imprisonment and even death?"

Much of their suffering was because some of them chose to go beyond what God required of them. They were so dedicated to preaching the Gospel that sometimes they openly walked into very dangerous situations, after being warned by the Holy Spirit.

52

Paul wrote to the church at Corinth and said, **There hath no temptation taken you but such as is common to man: but God is faithful, who will not suffer you to be tempted above that ye are able: but will with the temptation also make a way to escape, that ye may be able to bear it** (1 Cor. 10:13).

Paul made some decisions that caused him a lot of suffering and may have even been the cause of his death. He kept going to the Jews even though God sent him to the Gentiles. (Acts 22:17-21.) And nearly every time he preached to the Jews he was either stoned, beaten or thrown in jail. Here are the words of Paul before he went to Jerusalem the last time:

And now, behold, I go bound in the spirit unto Jerusalem, not knowing the things that shall befall me there:

Save that *the Holy Ghost witnesseth in every city, saying that bonds and afflictions abide me.*

But none of these things move me, neither count I my life dear unto myself, so that I might finish my course with joy, and the ministry, which I have received of the Lord Jesus, to testify the gospel of the grace of God.

And now, behold, I know that ye all, among whom I have gone preaching the kingdom of God, shall see my face no more.

Acts 20:22-25

He had revelation of the Holy Ghost every place he went of what would happen if he went to Jerusalem, and he went anyway.

A Way of Escape

In the city of Damascus, Paul escaped being killed by being let down a wall in a basket, as a garrison kept the city to kill him. God made a way of escape and he took it. (Acts 9:22-25.)

But in Acts twenty-one, Paul did not choose the way of escape, even though the prophet Agabus revealed what the Holy Ghost said would happen to Paul if he went to Jerusalem.

> **And as we tarried there many days, there came down from Judaea a certain prophet, named Agabus.**
>
> **And when he was come unto us, he took Paul's girdle, and bound his own hands and feet, and said, Thus saith the Holy Ghost, So shall the Jews at Jerusalem bind the man that owneth this girdle, and shall deliver him into the hands of the Gentiles.**
>
> **And when we heard these things, both we, and they of that place, besought him not to go up to Jerusalem.**
>
> **Then Paul answered, What mean ye to weep and to break mine heart? for I am ready not to be bound only, but also to die at Jerusalem for the name of the Lord Jesus.**
>
> Acts 21:10-13

Agabus told Paul what the Holy Ghost said about him going to Jerusalem. This warning came by supernatural revelation. In so many words Paul said, "That doesn't move me. I'm going anyway, even if it kills me."

Why would the Holy Ghost bring the same word of warning to him in every city if it was God's direction to go there? I believe Paul went beyond what God required of him. He had an option. God made a way of escape. But, Paul chose not to take it.

Paul's Decisions

We read in Philippians that Paul said, **For I am in a strait betwixt two, having a desire to depart, and to be with Christ; which is far better: Nevertheless to abide in the flesh is more needful for you** (Phil. 1:23,24). To paraphrase it, "I'd be better off if I'd go on to be with the Lord. But I guess, since you need me, I'll stay." Paul made a decision at that point and he stayed. But then, in Second Timothy Paul says,

> For *I am now ready to be offered*, and the time of my departure is at hand.
>
> I have fought a good fight, *I have finished my course,* I have kept the faith:
>
> Henceforth there is laid up for me a crown of righteousness....
>
> 2 Timothy 4:6-8

That was Paul's decision. They didn't take Paul's life. He gave it up after he had finished his work. He said, "I am *now* ready to be offered. I've done what God called me to do and now I'm ready to go."

Don't let the enemy make decisions for you. You should decide if you want to go or to stay. *You* may have to decree some things in faith in order to be able to see your way through your situation. Then the Lord will direct you. (Job 22:28; Prov. 16:9.)

Delivered Out of Them All

Before the apostle Paul died he gave this testimony to Timothy:

> But thou hast fully known my doctrine, manner of life, purpose, faith, longsuffering, charity, patience,
>
> Persecutions, afflictions, which came unto me at Antioch, at Iconium, at Lystra; what persecutions I endured: but out of them all the Lord delivered me.
>
> 2 Timothy 3:10,11

The messenger of Satan brought Paul many trials and persecutions. But Paul's testimony was **...out of them all the Lord delivered me.**

Messengers of Satan at Work Today

Paul is not the only one who ever had a thorn in the flesh. You may have a messenger of Satan sent against you. Even though your thorn or your buffeting may not be the same as what Paul experienced, there are still messengers of Satan assigned to buffet people today. They cause problems in their finances, in their physical bodies and in many other situations in life. Satan's goal is to keep you off balance physically, financially and spiritually so you can't fulfill your calling.

I would like to share some personal experiences I had several years ago because I believe it will relate to what many are experiencing in their lives today.

The Lord had called me into a teaching ministry. I was farming at the time. I began to have problems with the air conditioners. I had four air conditioners go out in my tractors. Our home air conditioner went out; then the air conditioner in my truck. The air conditioner in my car quit working. The air conditioner went out in the airplane. We went to a meeting and checked into a hotel and the air conditioner wouldn't work. The air conditioner wouldn't work at the church where we scheduled a meeting.

Then we went to another meeting, in Memphis. They sent a car to pick us up at the airport and the air conditioner was out in the car. Not only did the air conditioning not work, but before we got to the hotel the car quit and we had to catch a taxi.

In Mark 4:15-17, Jesus tells us that Satan uses afflictions and persecutions to get the Word out of you. The word "afflictions" means *pressures of life*. It really does not mean sickness but that could be included as pressures of life, for Satan will use anything that will put pressure on you to get you off the Word out of faith.

We left Memphis and flew to Tulsa and checked into a hotel room. When we got our bags unpacked we discovered the air conditioner was not working. While they were moving us to another room we decided to go out and eat.

We drove across town to a restaurant and the restaurant air conditioner went out. I was sitting there saying, "I'm seeing this. I know it's happening, but it's hard to believe that all of these things are happening one right after another."

The anointing of God came over me and I said to my wife, "This is satanic. This is a design of Satan, an angel of the devil dispatched to cause problems everywhere we go."

When we got back to the hotel, we began to exercise authority over the devil and all that had been assigned against us. We took authority over the messenger of Satan, broke his power of deception with the name of Jesus and dismissed him from his assignment. The problems stopped that day.

Although that was not a thorn in the flesh in the same sense as Paul's, it continually buffeted us until we took authority over that assignment Satan had sent against us.

God Allows What You Allow

It was not the will of God for all those things to happen to us, but God didn't do a thing about it until

57

we decided to act on the authority of His Word and stop it. It was not God's responsibility to stop it. But our God-given authority — linked with the anointing of the Holy Spirit and the name of Jesus — put a stop to it.

But an individual who believes whatever happens to them in life is God's will for them will never put up any resistance, and Satan will have his way in their lives rather than God. So don't let the devil deceive you into believing that everything that happens to you in life is God's will for you because it is simply not true. Remember Paul wrote to the Thessalonian Church and said, **We would have come unto you, even I Paul, once and again; but Satan hindered us** (1 Thess. 2:18).

There are many Christians who don't understand why these things happen to them. They usually ask, "Why is God allowing all of these things to happen to me?"

All they know to do is pray for God to do something about it. The answer Paul received will be the same answer they will receive from God, *"My grace is sufficient for you."* God's grace is always sufficient for every situation.

But there must be some action on our part. We were praying and waiting on God to do something. God was waiting on us, wondering why we hadn't taken authority over that angel of the devil, wondering why we hadn't dismissed him from his assignment. But until we acted on God's Word, He couldn't.

The Devil Flees

The victory was won by linking our authority with God's anointing, and the messenger was dismissed from his assignment. That doesn't mean that we didn't ever have any more problems with air conditioners, for man-made things do wear out with time. But we have never had any problems of that magnitude again.

Some of you reading this book need to exercise authority over the messenger of Satan that has been assigned to cause you trouble. If you will walk in FAITH and LOVE, the anointing that abides in you will teach you what you need to know about your situation. You have the authority and God will furnish the anointing to give you victory in your situation. But you have to make the decision to act on what you know; no one else can do it for you.

Thorns Are a Curse, Not a Blessing

Until you recognize your buffeting as being a messenger of Satan, you may never resist him. If you believe God sent this buffeting to you, you won't resist it.

Some people will have a thorn in the flesh all of their lives. Not because it's God's will, but because they simply don't know who is behind it. It certainly wasn't God's will for this revelation — that God had given Paul — to be hindered. Yet, it was hindered severely until Paul acted on his authority with God's anointing.

You Act and God Will Act

God wants you free, but unless you exercise your authority, God will not act alone on your behalf. Whatever you bind on earth will be bound in heaven (Matt. 16:19), but it must be bound on earth first.

If you ask the Lord to take your problems away, He is going to say to you what He said to Paul, "*My grace is sufficient for you."* Yes, He is willing *to use His power and His ability on your behalf, but first you must act on the authority of His Word to set that grace in motion.*

The good news is that you have been delivered from the authority of darkness and you are more than a conqueror through Jesus Christ. So don't wait six months to act on your God-given authority. As far as God is concerned, Satan is defeated, but you must enforce his defeat to stay free. (Col. 1:13; Rom. 8:37; James 4:7.)

Charles Capps is a retired farmer, land developer and ordained minister who travels throughout the United States sharing the truth of God's Word. He has taught Bible seminars for twenty-four years sharing how Christians can apply the Word to the circumstances of life and live victoriously.

In the mid '90s the Lord gave Charles an assignment to teach end-time events and a revelation of the coming of the Lord.

Besides authoring several books, including the best selling *The Tongue, A Creative Force,* and the minibook *God's Creative Power,* which has sold 2.8 million copies, Charles Capps Ministries has a national daily syndicated radio broadcast called "Concepts of Faith."

For a brochure of books
and tapes by Charles Capps, write:

Charles Capps Ministries
Box 69
England, AR 72046
Office phone: 501-842-2576 • Fax 501-842-2103

www.charlescapps.com

Order Toll-Free 1-877-396-9400

Books by Charles Capps